Team Spirit®

THE BOSTON BRUINS

BY

MARK STEWART

Content Consultant
Denis Gibbons
Society for International Hockey Research

NORWOOD HOUSE PRESS

CHICAGO, ILLINOIS

Norwood House Press
P.O. Box 316598
Chicago, Illinois 60631

For information regarding Norwood House Press, please visit our website at:
www.norwoodhousepress.com or call 866-565-2900.

PHOTO CREDITS:
All photos courtesy Getty Images except the following:
O-Pee-Chee Ltd. (6, 40 top), Sport Revue (7),
Esso/Imperial Oil Ltd. (9), McDiarmid/Cartophilium (14, 16),
Topps, Inc. (17, 23, 34 left, 35 top left, 37, 39), Associated Press (19, 27, 31),
Author's Collection (21, 41 left), Boy Scouts of America (22), Parade Sportive (28),
Bee Hive Golden Corn Syrup/Cargill, Inc. (34 bottom right, 43),
Goudey Gum Co. (40 bottom), Imperial Tobacco (41 right).
Cover photo: Elsa/Getty Images
Special thanks to Topps, Inc.

Editor: Mike Kennedy
Designer: Ron Jaffe
Project Management: Black Book Partners, LLC.
Research: Joshua Zaffos
Special thanks Michael Broderick

LIBRARY OF CONGRESS CATALOGING-IN-PUBLICATION DATA

Stewart, Mark, 1960-
  The Boston Bruins / by Mark Stewart.
    p. cm. -- (Team spirit)
  Includes bibliographical references and index.
  Summary: "Presents the history and accomplishments of the Boston Bruins
hockey team. Includes highlights of players, coaches, and awards, quotes,
timeline, maps, glossary, and websites"--Provided by publisher.
  ISBN-13: 978-1-59953-399-5 (library edition : alk. paper)
  ISBN-10: 1-59953-399-5 (library edition : alk. paper)
  1. Boston Bruins (Hockey team)--History--Juvenile literature. I. Title.
  GV848.B6.S74 2011
  796.962'640974461--dc22
                                        2010010625

Manufactured in the United States of America in North Mankato, Minnesota.
159N—072010

COVER PHOTO: The players on Boston's bench celebrate a goal during a 2009–10 game.

Table of Contents

SPORTS WORDS & VOCABULARY WORDS: In this book, you will find many words that are new to you. You may also see familiar words used in new ways. The glossary on page 46 gives the meanings of hockey words, as well as "everyday" words that have special hockey meanings. These words appear in **bold type** throughout the book. The glossary on page 47 gives the meanings of vocabulary words that are not related to hockey. They appear in ***bold italic type*** throughout the book.

Meet the Bruins

F ew animals are faster or scarier than an angry bear. That is why Boston fans say their team has the perfect name. *Bruin* is another name for a Brown Bear. The Bruins were the first team from the United States to join the **National Hockey League (NHL)** and one of four of the league's "Original Six" clubs from south of the Canadian border. They found success almost immediately and have thrilled *generations* of hockey fans in New England ever since.

The Bruins like to build their teams around players with unusual talents. Sometimes that player is a superstar who can control the game all by himself. Sometimes he is a **role player** who finds amazing ways to make his teammates better. The same goes for the people who run the Bruins. They find talent where others fail to look.

This book tells the story of the Bruins. They win games by mixing strong defense with powerful skating and shooting. They win championships when they have a dressing room full of *dynamic* players. They win fans by playing hard and never giving up.

Boston captain Zdeno Chara stands tall as the Bruins celebrate a goal during the 2009–10 season.

Way Back When

In the early 1920s, the National Hockey League was only "national" in Canada. There were no teams that played in the U.S. That changed in 1924, when the Boston Bruins joined the league. The NHL soon had an entire American Division, which included teams in Chicago, Pittsburgh, Detroit, and New York.

EDDIE SHORE
BOSTON "BRUINS"—Defence
LITHOGRAPHED IN CANADA
100

Boston won only six games during the 1924–25 season. However, by the end of the *decade*, the Bruins were one of the top NHL teams. They reached the **Stanley Cup Finals** three times in four years and won the championship once. Boston's stars included Cooney Weiland, Dit Clapper, Harry Oliver, Lionel Hitchman, and Cecil "Tiny" Thompson.

The player who made the Bruins roar was Eddie Shore. Boston fans loved him, and fans in other cities loved to boo him. After warm-ups in Boston Garden, Shore would remain on the ice. The lights would go dark, and he would skate into the spotlight. The organist would play "Hail to the Chief "—the same song played for the President of the United States.

Shore was no longer on the team when the Bruins won the **Stanley Cup** in 1939 and 1941. Those clubs were led by Milt Schmidt, Woody Dumart, and Bobby Bauer. Other stars included goalie Frank Brimsek, **playmaker** Bill Cowley, and Roy Conacher, who topped the NHL in scoring as a **rookie** in 1938–39.

During the 1950s and 1960s, the Bruins put more fine players on the ice. One of their best was a rugged defenseman named Fern Flaman. Three others—Johnny Bucyk, Vic Stasiuk, and Rudy "Bronco" Horvath—formed a high-scoring line. They helped the Bruins reach the Stanley Cup Finals in 1958.

In 1966–67, a young defenseman named Bobby Orr joined the team. Orr was a superstar from the moment he began his NHL career. Not long after Orr arrived, the Bruins made a great trade for Phil Esposito, Ken Hodge, and Fred Stanfield. Starting in 1967–68, Boston reached the **playoffs** each season for 29 years in a row. They soon became known as the "Big Bad Bruins."

LEFT: Eddie Shore, one of the most beloved players in team history.
ABOVE: This 1960 magazine features Vic Stasiuk and Bronco Horvath on the cover.

Orr became the first defenseman to top 100 points (goals plus **assists**) in a season. Esposito set an NHL record with 76 goals in 1970–71. They teamed up with Wayne Cashman, Ed Westfall, Derek Sanderson, Dallas Smith, and goalie Gerry Cheevers. Boston reached the Stanley Cup Finals five times during the 1970s and won the championship twice.

Raymond BOURQUE

In the 1980s, the Bruins welcomed a new group of leaders. Terry O'Reilly, Rick Middleton, Barry Pederson, Pete Peeters, Peter McNab, Cam Neely, and Ray Bourque ranked among the top players in the NHL. Bourque stood out as an all-time great. He reminded some fans around the league of Orr.

Bourque helped the Bruins reach the Stanley Cup Finals in 1987–88, and once again in 1989–90. In both seasons, Boston defeated the Montreal Canadiens in the playoffs. It was a sweet feeling because the teams had a heated *rivalry*. Still, beating the Canadiens did not replace the thrill of winning another Stanley Cup. Boston fans ached to see the Bruins hold the trophy high once again.

LEFT: Bobby Orr looks for an opening in the defense.
ABOVE: A trading card of Ray Bourque, who followed in Orr's footsteps.

The Team Today

In 1996–97, the Bruins missed the playoffs for the first time since the 1960s. Boston began rebuilding around talented new players such as Joe Thornton, Jason Allison, and Sergei Samsonov. They helped the team return to its winning ways, but Boston did not make it back to the Stanley Cup Finals.

The Bruins finally chose to replace these stars. Many fans thought this *strategy* was a mistake—especially after Thornton won the Hart Trophy as the league's **Most Valuable Player (MVP)** with the San Jose Sharks. Meanwhile, the other sports teams in New England all won championships. The Bruins were under pressure to do the same.

In 2008–09, Boston rediscovered the winning *formula*. Coach Claude Julien mixed **veterans** Zdeno Chara, Tim Thomas, and P.J. Axelsson with young players like Tuukka Rask, Milan Lucic, and Patrice Bergeron. At season's end, Boston had the best record in the NHL's **Eastern Conference**. The Bruins continued their fine play in 2009–10. The team and its fans were confident that they could return to the glory years of the "Big Bad Bruins."

Boston fans cheer for P.J. Axelsson and Patrice Bergeron after a goal in a 2008–09 game.

11

Home Ice

For most of their time in the NHL, the Bruins played their home games in Boston Garden. The arena was built for boxing matches. For hockey games, this meant that many seats were close to the ice and fans got amazing close-up views of the action. For visiting players, Boston Garden could be confusing. Not only were the fans right on top of them, but the rink itself was several feet shorter than others in the NHL.

In 1995, the Bruins moved into a new arena that some fans still call "The Garden." Like the old building, it sits atop Boston's North Station. Fans can reach the arena by train or bus from almost anywhere in Massachusetts. Many simply walk to games from the surrounding neighborhoods.

BY THE NUMBERS

- *The team's arena has 17,565 seats for hockey.*
- *The "old" Garden and "new" Garden were built only nine inches apart.*
- *As of 2009–10, the Bruins have retired 10 numbers: 2 (Eddie Shore), 3 (Lionel Hitchman), 4 (Bobby Orr), 5 (Dit Clapper), 7 (Phil Esposito), 8 (Cam Neely), 9 (Johnny Bucyk), 15 (Milt Schmidt), 24 (Terry O'Reilly), and 77 (Ray Bourque).*

Banners from the Bruins' championship seasons and retired numbers of famous players hang from the ceiling of the team's arena.

Dressed for Success

Boston's first official colors were brown and gold. These were also the colors used by Finast Foods. That was the grocery store chain owned by Charles Adams, the owner of the Bruins.

Boston switched to black and gold during the 1930s. Also during that decade, the Bruins began using a large *B* on the front of their uniforms. In the 1940s, a circle was added around this ***logo***. The team has made small changes to its uniform since then.

When the Bruins play at home, they usually wear a black sweater with black sleeves and gold around the shoulders. On the road, the players often wear a white sweater with a black band and black sleeves. Sometimes the Bruins wear a special black road uniform. It shows a bear and also has the name of the team and city on the front.

Cooney Weiland models the Boston uniform when the team colors were brown and gold.

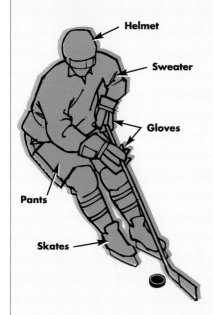

The hockey uniform has five important parts:
- Helmet
- Sweater
- Pants
- Gloves
- Skates

Hockey helmets are made of hard plastic with softer padding inside. Some players also wear visors to protect their eyes.

The hockey uniform top is called a sweater. Players wear padding underneath it to protect their shoulders, spine and ribs. Padded hockey pants, or "breezers," extend from the waist to the knees. Players also wear padding on their knees and shins.

Hockey gloves protect the top of the hand and the wrist. Only a thin layer of leather covers the palm, which helps a player control his stick. A goalie wears two different gloves—one for catching pucks and one for blocking them. Goalies also wear heavy leg pads and a mask. They paint their masks to match their personalities and team colors.

All players wear hockey skates. The blade is curved at each end. The skate top is made from metal, plastic, nylon, and either real or *synthetic* leather. Goalies wear skates that have extra protection on the toe and ankle.

Dave Krejci wears the team's 2009–10 home uniform.

We Won!

In the early days of the NHL, there were a lot of very good players but only a handful of teams. Every club, from first down to worst, could put stars on the ice. That made the Stanley Cup Finals very competitive. For example, in 1929–30, the Bruins went 38–5–1. No team has ever won a higher percentage of games in a season. Yet the Bruins fell to the Montreal Canadiens in the Stanley Cup Finals.

In the years the Bruins did win the championship, they needed help from every player on the team. In 1928–29, they beat the New York Rangers in a best-of-three series. Their star was rookie goalie Tiny Thompson. He stopped all but one of the shots New York fired at him. With the young netminder playing like an old **pro**, the Bruins won two close games on goals by Dit Clapper and Bill Carson.

Ten years later, the Bruins returned to the top of the NHL. They beat the Rangers in the opening round of the playoffs, but some New York fans are still wondering how. The Rangers were in control of six

of the seven games played between the two teams. The difference for Boston was Mel Hill, who ended three games with goals in **overtime**. The exhausted Bruins went on to beat the Toronto Maple Leafs in the finals in five games.

The Bruins had an easier time in 1940–41, when they defeated the Detroit Red Wings for the Stanley Cup. Boston fans were more worried about the series before that, against the Toronto Maple Leafs. During the opening game, Boston star Bill Cowley and Toronto's Sweeney Schriner collided on the ice. Cowley was hurt and forced to the bench, but the Bruins still beat the Maple Leafs.

The following series against the Red Wings was fun for the Bruins and their fans. Detroit decided to play fast, wide-open hockey. That was a mistake. Boston loved that style of play. Each contest was close, but the Bruins won four in a row. Milt Schmidt and Roy Conacher each broke a tie with a game-winning goal.

The next time the Bruins held the Stanley Cup high was at the end of the 1969–70 season. The NHL had grown to a dozen teams.

Boston had the game's best player, Bobby Orr. He led a powerful offense that included Phil Esposito, John McKenzie, Johnny Bucyk, and Derek Sanderson.

The Bruins skated against the St. Louis Blues in the Stanley Cup Finals. Scotty Bowman, the coach of the Blues, knew his team faced a stiff challenge. "We practiced covering Bobby Orr for six hours today," Bowman joked at one point. "But the only trouble is, we don't have a Bobby Orr to practice against!"

The Bruins won the first three games easily. When the final game of the series went into overtime, everyone expected Orr to make the winning play. He came through with the Cup-winning goal to complete a four-game sweep of the Blues.

Orr was the star again when Boston won its fifth Stanley Cup, in 1971–72. With the Bruins leading the Rangers three games to two in the finals, he scored early in Game 6 to give his team the lead. Goalie Gerry Cheevers took over from there. He made one save after another to hold New York scoreless. Wayne Cashman pumped in two goals to make the final score 3–0. Just as in 1970, Orr was awarded the Conn Smythe Trophy as the MVP of the playoffs.

LEFT: Phil Esposito glides toward the net against the St. Louis Blues.
ABOVE: Johnny Bucyk skates with the Stanley Cup in 1971–72.

Go-To Guys

To be a true star in the NHL, you need more than a great slapshot. You have to be a "go-to guy"—someone teammates trust to make the winning play when the seconds are ticking away in a big game. Bruins fans have had a lot to cheer about over the years, including these great stars ...

THE PIONEERS

EDDIE SHORE   Defenseman

• BORN: 11/25/1902 • DIED: 3/16/1985 • PLAYED FOR TEAM: 1926–27 TO 1939–40

Eddie Shore had the speed and skill of a forward, but he was tough enough to be a defenseman. This made him hockey's best "two-way" player. Shore paid a high price for his *aggressiveness*—he needed more than 900 stitches throughout his career to close his many wounds.

DIT CLAPPER   Right Wing/Defenseman

• BORN: 2/9/1907 • DIED: 1/21/1978 • PLAYED FOR TEAM: 1927–28 TO 1946–47

Dit Clapper was a great player for a long time. In fact, the NHL put him in the **Hall of Fame** the night he retired. Clapper was the first player to wear the same team's uniform for 20 seasons.

TINY THOMPSON   Goalie

• BORN: 5/31/1905 • DIED: 2/9/1981 • PLAYED FOR TEAM: 1928–29 TO 1938–39

Cecil "Tiny" Thompson got his nickname as a joke during his youth hockey days. He was actually the tallest player on his team! Thompson was a master at the **glove save**.

BILL COWLEY   Center

• BORN: 6/12/1912 • DIED: 12/31/1993 • PLAYED FOR TEAM: 1935–36 TO 1946–47

Bill Cowley was a swift and smart skater. His pinpoint passes made the Bruins hard to defend. Despite missing many games due to injury, Cowley retired from the NHL with the all-time record for points.

MILT SCHMIDT   Center

• BORN: 3/5/1918 • PLAYED FOR TEAM: 1936–37 TO 1954–55

Milt Schmidt always found a way to make his linemates better. In 1950–51, the Bruins had a losing record. But Schmidt was so good that he was awarded the Hart Trophy as the NHL MVP.

FRANK BRIMSEK   Goalie

• BORN: 9/26/1915 • DIED: 11/11/1998
• PLAYED FOR TEAM: 1938–39 TO 1948–49

Frank Brimsek had **shutouts** in six of his first eight NHL games. By the end of his rookie season, Brimsek had won the **Vezina Trophy**, **Calder Trophy**, and Stanley Cup. He also had a new nickname: "Mr. Zero."

Frank Brimsek

JOHNNY BUCYK **Left Wing**

• BORN: 5/12/1935 • PLAYED FOR TEAM: 1957–58 TO 1977–78

Johnny Bucyk used his great size to deliver crunching checks and power the puck into the net. The older he got, the more he scored. At the age of 35, Bucyk became the oldest player ever to reach the 50-goal mark in one season.

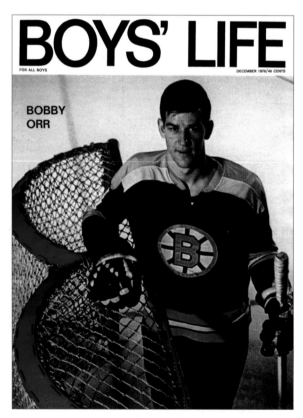

BOBBY ORR **Defenseman**

• BORN: 3/20/1948

• PLAYED FOR TEAM: 1966–67 TO 1975–76

Bobby Orr turned the Bruins from a losing team into an NHL powerhouse. He was the best player anyone had ever seen. In 1970–71, Orr had a record-setting **plus/minus rating** of +124.

PHIL ESPOSITO **Center**

• BORN: 2/20/1942

• PLAYED FOR TEAM: 1967–68 TO 1975–76

A big body and lightning-quick reflexes made Phil Esposito impossible to stop when he found a spot near the net. "Espo" topped 100 points five years in a row. He won the Hart Trophy twice during his nine seasons as a Bruin.

RAY BOURQUE   Defenseman

• Born: 12/28/1960   • Played for Team: 1979–80 to 1999–00

Ray Bourque used his terrific skating and shooting to control the pace of the game. Few defensemen have ever done this as well as he did. As a rookie, Bourque was the first player at his position ever to win the Calder Trophy and be named a First-Team **All-Star**.

CAM NEELY   Right Wing

• Born: 6/6/1965

• Played for Team: 1986–87 to 1995–96

Cam Neely was one of the scariest players in hockey. He had a hard, accurate shot and a short temper, and no one ever outworked him. Neely scored goals like crazy. In 1993–94, he was injured but still netted 50 goals in 49 games.

ZDENO CHARA   Defenseman

• Born: 3/18/1977   • First Season with Team: 2006–07

In the early years of the NHL, no one could have imagined a player like Zdeno Chara. When the Bruins signed him, he was the tallest player in league history at 6′ 9″. Chara moved with great *agility* and had the NHL's hardest slapshot.

LEFT: Bobby Orr poses for the cover of this Boy Scouts magazine. He was a hero to millions of young fans.   **ABOVE**: Cam Neely

23

Behind the Bench

Few teams in any sport can claim as many *legendary* coaches as the Bruins. Their first coach, Art Ross, actually named the team—and then oversaw three Stanley Cup championships from behind the bench and as a team *executive*. Superstars Cy Denneny and Cooney Weiland also guided the Bruins to the Stanley Cup in the team's early years. Other former players who led the Bruins to glory were Dit Clapper and Milt Schmidt.

In 1966–67, the Bruins were the youngest team in the NHL. That included their coach, Harry Sinden. Three years later, Sinden guided the team to its fourth Stanley Cup. He left the Bruins and coached Team Canada in a 1972 series against the Soviet Union. Sinden later returned to Boston to run the team's business affairs.

Tom Johnson coached the Bruins to their fifth Stanley Cup in 1971–72. He was followed by other top coaches, including Don Cherry and Pat Burns. Both won the Jack Adams Award as the NHL's top coach. In 2008–09, Claude Julien led the Bruins to 53 victories and a division championship. He became the team's third Jack Adams Award winner.

Claude Julien congratulates his players after a goal during the 2010 playoffs.

One Great Day

During the 1960s, winning the Stanley Cup seemed like a faraway dream for Boston fans. Most years, their team finished last or next-to-last in the standings. In the spring of 1970, however, the Bruins made the playoffs and were on a roll. They defeated the New York Rangers in a rowdy series and then swept the Chicago Blackhawks in four straight games. The only team left to beat for the Stanley Cup was the St. Louis Blues.

The Bruins were led by Bobby Orr, who was the NHL's scoring champ with 120 points. No defenseman had ever claimed that honor before. Right behind him, in second place in scoring, was Phil Esposito. Together, they helped Boston easily win the first three games against the Blues. Game 4 was a different matter.

The Bruins attacked the St. Louis net all game. They scored three times, but the Blues netted three goals of their own. The game went into overtime.

Boston fans barely had time to settle back into their seats when Orr streaked toward the St. Louis net. He passed to Derek Sanderson and

The camera catches Bobby Orr flying through the air after his game-winning goal.

then glided to the goal. Sanderson slid the puck back to Orr, who whacked it past goalie Glenn Hall. As Orr shot, he was tripped. Orr was still in midair when the goal light flashed on, and he raised his arms in celebration. He had already won the **Norris Trophy**, Hart Trophy, and **Art Ross Trophy**. His amazing goal guaranteed a fourth award—the Conn Smythe Trophy as MVP of the playoffs.

Legend Has It

Which Bruin's honesty cost him an NHL scoring title?

PARADE SPORTIVE
PAUL STUART
LE PREMIER PROGRAMME DU GENRE
Interviews des Célébrités de tous les Sports   Correspondance: 4314 St-André, Montréal, 34
SPORTez-vous bien !

Bill COWLEY

LEGEND HAS IT that Bill Cowley did. After a 1942–43 game against the New York Rangers, Cowley told NHL officials that he did not deserve an assist that was on the scoresheet. The league took the assist away. At the end of the year, Cowley finished with 27 goals and 45 assists for a total of 72 points—one less than the NHL scoring champ, Doug Bentley. The "missing assist" also prevented Cowley from breaking his own league record for assists. To make matters worse, the Bruins had promised Cowley a bonus if he had 46 assists or more, so he also lost some money. Cowley retired four seasons later after playing 549 games. He had 548 career points. Cowley had no regrets about his missing assist.

Who brought the first aluminum sticks to the NHL?

LEGEND HAS IT that Brad Park did. In 1979, Park showed up at a Boston practice with a stick that had an aluminum shaft. It was made by Sher-Wood, a company that already supplied sticks to many NHL players. The stick had an opening on the bottom where a wooden blade could be attached. Park wasn't allowed to use the stick in games. The league did not approve aluminum sticks until the 1982–83 season.

Who was the NHL's "streakiest" goalie?

LEGEND HAS IT that Gerry Cheevers was. But not all Boston fans agree. During one stretch in the 1971–72 season, Cheevers set an NHL record with a 32-game unbeaten streak. In all, he won 24 games and recorded eight more ties without a loss. In 1975–76, Gilles Gilbert won 17 games in a row for the Bruins. Whose streak is the best? Fans are still arguing about that one.

LEFT: Bill Cowley
ABOVE: Brad Park

It Really Happened

When the 1938–39 season began, Mel Hill was unknown to most NHL fans, even in Boston. Hill was just another young player fighting for ice time. By the end of the season, he was practically a household name.

Hill scored 10 goals that year and helped the Bruins finish with the best record in the NHL. Still, he was just a "spare part" when the Bruins faced the New York Rangers in the playoffs. The Bruins had a strong team, and everyone expected them to capture the Stanley Cup without much of a problem.

The Rangers put up a great fight. In Game 1, the score was tied 1–1 after 60 minutes. Two overtime periods passed without either team scoring. Finally, in the third overtime, Bill Cowley passed to Hill, and he lifted a shot into the net to win the game. Two nights later, the Bruins and Rangers were tied 2–2 after three periods. Once again, Hill ended the game with an overtime goal.

The Rangers would not quit. They won three of the next four games to set up an exciting Game 7. No one was surprised when neither club could break a 1–1 tie.

Mel "Sudden Death" Hill scrambles on the ice for a loose puck in the 1940–41 Stanley Cup Finals. He had earned his nickname two years earlier.

In the third overtime, Cowley controlled the puck behind the New York net. He saw Hill open at the mouth of the goal. Cowley put a pass right on his stick. Hill flipped the puck over the goalie to win the series—and the Bruins went on to win the Stanley Cup against the Toronto Maple Leafs. From that day on, Hill was known as "Sudden Death."

"I was a basic, unspectacular player who usually performed well when it counted," Hill said. "I just happened to get super-hot in that series with New York."

Team Spirit

How good are Bruins fans? Wicked good! They know their players and their team history, and they understand hockey almost as well as the referees. They make Boston's home ice truly feel like home. And they can make visiting players very uncomfortable.

The Bruins have many *traditions*—and the team keeps adding to them. In 2010, Boston beat the Philadelphia Flyers in an outdoor game called the Winter Classic at baseball's Fenway Park. Patrice Bergeron and Marco Sturm teamed up to win the game in overtime. Afterwards, the Bruins raised their sticks together to salute the fans.

Although it doesn't take much to get Bruins fans cheering, the club finds a lot of different ways to keep the crowd entertained. Blades, the team *mascot*, is a man in a big, cuddly bear suit. He loves to slide around the rink and roam around the stands. Blades shares the arena with the Ice Girls, the Bruins' dance team.

The Bruins salute their fans after the 2010 Winter Classic.

Timeline

The hockey season is played from October through June. That means each season takes place at the end of one year and the beginning of the next. In this timeline, the accomplishments of the Bruins are shown by season.

1924–25
Boston becomes the first U.S. city in the NHL.

1943–44
Herb Cain sets a record with 82 points in 48 games.

1928–29
The Bruins win their first Stanley Cup.

1959–60
Bronco Horvath ties for the NHL lead in goals.

1966–67
Bobby Orr wins the Calder Trophy.

ALL-TIME GREATS

DIT CLAPPER

Dit Clapper, a star for the 1928–29 champs.

Bronco Horvath

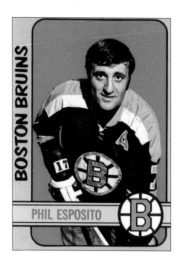

Phil
Esposito

Ray
Bourque

1973–74
Phil Esposito wins the scoring
title for the fourth year in a row.

1990–91
Ray Bourque sets a record with
19 shots on goal in one game.

1982–83
Pete Peeters wins
the Vezina Trophy.

2008–09
Zdeno Chara sets a
record with a 105.4 mph
(169.62 kph) slapshot.

2009–10
The Bruins win
the Winter Classic.

Zdeno Chara fires his
record-setting slapshot.

Fun Facts

IN STITCHES

The first NHL goalie to decorate his mask was Gerry Cheevers. He painted "Frankenstein stitches" over the spots where pucks would have cut his face. Cheevers filled up four masks before his career was over!

BREAKING BARRIERS

On January 18, 1958, the Bruins called up Willie O'Ree from the **minor leagues**. When he took the ice against the Montreal Canadiens that night, he became the first black player in NHL history. In 2008, the NHL celebrated the 50th anniversary of that moment in Boston and later at the **All-Star Game**.

POWER-LESS

In 1977–78, Stan Jonathan had 27 goals for the Bruins without scoring on the **power play**. His team record lasted exactly one year. In 1978–79, John Wensink scored 28 times without a power-play goal.

IRON MAN

In 1963–64, Eddie Johnston played every minute of all 70 games for the Bruins. The super-tough goalie broke his nose several times—and twice doctors had to use leeches to drain blood from his eyes so that he could see!

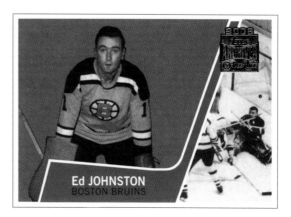

RAISING CAIN

During the 1940s, most of the NHL's top players were serving in World War II. Those who remained in the league often faced poor competition. In 1943–44, Herb Cain set a record with 82 points in only 48 games. He never had more than 45 points in any other season for the Bruins.

YOUNG STAR

In 2006–07, 19-year-old Phil Kessel was diagnosed with cancer. He beat the disease and returned to the ice for the Bruins that season. In the 2007 **YoungStars game**, Kessel scored a **hat trick**!

LEFT: Gerry Cheevers shows off one of his "stitches" masks.
ABOVE: A trading card of Eddie Johnston.

Talking Hockey

"Forget about style. Worry about results."

—Bobby Orr, on the importance of winning

"He was two steps ahead of anyone, and then after his knee injury he was one step ahead."

—Brad Park, on the speed of Bobby Orr

"There has to be a balance between confidence and respect. It's good to have confidence against a team, but you also have to play them hard and with respect."

—Zdeno Chara, on the danger of being overconfident in the NHL

"Getting to the Stanley Cup Finals twice was quite a highlight. But on the other hand, it was also disappointing to get that far and not win the championship."

—Cam Neely, on the best and worst moments of his career

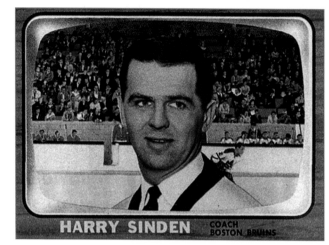

Harry Sinden

"If I'm down a goal late in the game, I want Orr on the ice. If I'm up a goal late in the game, Bourque's the one I want out there."

—Harry Sinden, on the difference between his two Hall of Fame defensemen

"My philosophy has always been that the other team can fill the net on me—as long as we get one more goal."

—Gerry Cheevers, on

"It wasn't an easy tag to carry the rest of my c̶ I was expected to be the hero in every playo̶ moment on."

—Mel Hill, on h̶ Sudden Death"

"Stay positive and bear down in games."

—Patrice Bergeron, on the key to playing good hockey

For the Record

The great Bruins teams and players have left their marks on the record books. These are the "best of the best" …

Eddie Shore

BRUINS AWARD WINNERS

VEZINA TROPHY
TOP GOALTENDER

Tiny Thompson	1929–30
Tiny Thompson	1932–33
Tiny Thompson	1935–36
Tiny Thompson	1937–38
Frank Brimsek	1938–39
Frank Brimsek	1941–42
Pete Peeters	1982–83
Tim Thomas	2008–09

JAMES NORRIS MEMORIAL TROPHY
TOP DEFENSIVE PLAYER

Orr	1967–68
Orr	1968–69
Orr	1969–70
Orr	1970–71
	1971–72
	1972–73
	1973–74
	1974–75
	1986–87
	1987–88
Ray Bourque	1989–90
Ray Bourque	1990–91
Ray Bourque	1993–94
Zdeno Chara	2008–09

CONN SMYTHE TROPHY
MVP DURING PLAYOFFS

Bobby Orr	1969–70
Bobby Orr	1971–72

CALDER TROPHY
TOP ROOKIE

Frank Brimsek	1938–39
Jack Gelineau	1949–50
Larry Regan	1956–57
Bobby Orr	1966–67
Derek Sanderson	1967–68
Ray Bourque	1979–80
Sergei Samsonov	1997–98
Andrew Raycroft	2003–04

ART ROSS TROPHY
TOP SCORER

Phil Esposito	1968–69
Bobby Orr	1969–70
Phil Esposito	1970–71
Phil Esposito	1971–72
Phil Esposito	1972–73
Phil Esposito	1973–74
Bobby Orr	1974–75

HART MEMORIAL TROPHY
MOST VALUABLE PLAYER

Eddie Shore	1932–33
Eddie Shore	1934–35
Eddie Shore	1935–36
Eddie Shore	1937–38
Bill Cowley	1940–41
Bill Cowley	1942–43
Milt Schmidt	1950–51
Phil Esposito	1968–69
Bobby Orr	1969–70
Bobby Orr	1970–71
Bobby Orr	1971–72
Phil Esposito	1973–74

BRUINS ACHIEVEMENTS

ACHIEVEMENT	YEAR
Stanley Cup Finalists	1926–27
Stanley Cup Champions	1928–29
Stanley Cup Finalists	1929–30
Stanley Cup Champions	1938–39
Stanley Cup Champions	1940–41
Stanley Cup Finalists	1942–43
Stanley Cup Finalists	1945–46
Stanley Cup Finalists	1952–53
Stanley Cup Finalists	1956–57
Stanley Cup Finalists	1957–58
Stanley Cup Champions	1969–70
Stanley Cup Champions	1971–72
Stanley Cup Finalists	1973–74
Stanley Cup Finalists	1976–77
Stanley Cup Finalists	1977–78
Stanley Cup Finalists	1987–88
Stanley Cup Finalists	1989–90

... worn by Bruins fans during the 1950s.
ABOVE: Art Ross, Boston's first coach and the leader of the team's first three Stanley Cup winners.

Pinpoints

The history of a hockey team is made up of many smaller stories. These stories take place all over the map—not just in the city a team calls "home." Match the pushpins on these maps to the Team Facts and you will begin to see the story of the Bruins unfold!

TEAM FACTS

1 Boston, Massachusetts—*The Bruins have played here since 1924–25.*

2 Flint, Michigan—*Tim Thomas was born here.*

3 Madison, Wisconsin—*Phil Kessel was born here.*

4 Eveleth, Minnesota—*Frank Brimsek was born here.*

5 Comox, British Columbia, Canada—*Cam Neely was born here.*

6 Edmonton, Alberta, Canada—*Johnny Bucyk was born here.*

7 Dysart, Saskatchewan, Canada—*Fern Flaman was born here.*

8 Toronto, Ontario, Canada—*Lionel Hitchman was born here.*

9 Montreal, Quebec, Canada—*Ray Bourque was born here.*

10 Trencin, Czechoslovakia* —*Zdeno Chara was born here.*

11 Kungalv, Sweden—*P.J. Axelsson was born here.*

12 Moscow, Russia—*Sergei Samsonov was born here.*

* Now known as Slovakia.

Fern Flaman

Faceoff

Hockey is played between two teams of six skaters. Each team has a goalie, two defensemen, and a forward line that includes a left wing, right wing and center. The goalie's job is to stop the puck from crossing the red goal line. A hockey goal is six feet wide and four feet high. The hockey puck is a round disk made of hard rubber. It weighs approximately six ounces.

During a game, players skate as hard as they can for a full "shift." When they get tired, they take a seat on the bench, and a new group jumps off the bench and over the boards to take their place. Forwards play together in set groups, or "lines," and defensemen do too.

There are rules that prevent players from injuring or interfering with opponents. However, players are allowed to bump, or "check," each other when they battle for the puck. Because hockey is a fast game played by strong athletes, sometimes checks can be rough!

If a player breaks a rule, a penalty is called by the referee. For most penalties, the player must sit in the penalty box for two minutes. This gives the other team a one-skater advantage, or "power play." The team down a skater is said to be "short-handed."

NHL games have three 20-minute periods—60 minutes in all—and the team that scores the most goals when time has run out is the winner. If the score is tied, the teams play an overtime period. The first team to score during overtime wins. If the game is still tied, then it is decided by a shootout—a one-on-one contest between the goalies and the best shooters. During the Stanley Cup playoffs, no shootouts are held. The teams play until the tie is broken.

Things happen so quickly in hockey that it is easy to overlook set plays. The next time you watch a game, see if you can spot these plays:

 PLAY LIST

DEFLECTION—Sometimes a shooter does not try to score a goal. Instead, he aims his shot so that a teammate can touch the puck with his stick and suddenly change its direction. If the goalie is moving to stop the first shot, he may be unable to adjust to the "deflection."

GIVE-AND-GO—When a skater is closely guarded and cannot get an open shot, he sometimes passes to a teammate with the idea of getting a return pass in better position to shoot. The "give-and-go" works when the defender turns to follow the pass and loses track of his man. By the time he recovers, it is too late.

ONE-TIMER—When a player receives a pass, he must control the puck and position himself for a shot. This gives the defense a chance to react. Some players are skilled enough to shoot the instant a pass arrives for a "one-timer." A well-aimed one-timer is almost impossible to stop.

PULLING THE GOALIE—Sometimes in the final moments of a game, the team that is behind will try a risky play. To gain an extra skater, the team will pull the goalie out of the game and replace him with a center, wing, or defenseman. This gives the team a better chance to score. It also leaves the goal unprotected and allows the opponent to score an "empty-net goal."

Glossary

HOCKEY WORDS TO KNOW

ALL-STAR—An award given to the league's best players at the end of each season.

ALL-STAR GAME—The annual game featuring the NHL's best players.

ART ROSS TROPHY—The award given to the league's top scorer each season.

ASSISTS—Passes that lead to a goal.

CALDER TROPHY—The award given to the league's top rookie each season.

EASTERN CONFERENCE—A group of teams from the East. Each season, a team from the Eastern Conference faces a team from the Western Conference for the Stanley Cup.

GLOVE SAVE—A save made by a goalie in which he uses his catching glove to snatch the puck.

HALL OF FAME—The museum in Toronto, Ontario, Canada, where hockey's greatest players are honored. A player voted into the Hall of Fame is sometimes called a "Hall of Famer."

HAT TRICK—Three goals in one game.

MINOR LEAGUES—A level of play below the NHL.

MOST VALUABLE PLAYER (MVP)—The award given each year to the league's best player; also given to the best player in the playoffs and All-Star Game.

NATIONAL HOCKEY LEAGUE (NHL)—The league that began play in 1917–18 and is still in existence today.

NORRIS TROPHY—The award given to the league's top defenseman each season.

OVERTIME—The extra 20-minute period played when a game is tied after 60 minutes. Teams continue playing overtime periods until one team scores a goal and wins.

PLAYMAKER—A player who creates scoring opportunities.

PLAYOFFS—The games played after the season to determine the league champion.

PLUS/MINUS RATING—A statistic that measures a player's effectiveness by comparing the goals scored for and against his team when he's on the ice.

POWER PLAY—When one team has at least one extra player on the ice because of a penalty.

PRO—A player or team that plays a sport for money. Also, a term for a player with great experience.

ROLE PLAYER—A player who has a specific job when he is on the ice.

ROOKIE—A player in his first season.

SHUTOUTS—Games in which a team is prevented from scoring.

STANLEY CUP—The championship trophy of North American hockey since 1893, and of the NHL since 1927.

STANLEY CUP FINALS—The series that determines the NHL champion each season. It has been a best-of-seven series since 1939.

VETERANS—Players with great experience.

VEZINA TROPHY—The award given to the league's top goalie each season.

YOUNGSTARS GAME—A game between the NHL's best young players, held the day before the All-Star Game.

OTHER WORDS TO KNOW

AGGRESSIVENESS—Being bold or powerful.

AGILITY—Quickness and grace.

DECADE—A period of 10 years; also specific periods, such as the 1950s.

DYNAMIC—Exciting and energetic.

EXECUTIVE—A person who makes important decisions for a company.

FORMULA—A set way of doing something.

GENERATIONS—Periods of years roughly equal to the time it takes for a person to be born, grow up, and have children.

LEGENDARY—Famous.

LOGO—A symbol or design that represents a company or team.

MASCOT—An animal or person believed to bring a group good luck.

RIVALRY—Extremely emotional competition.

STRATEGY—A plan or method for succeeding.

SYNTHETIC—Made in a laboratory, not in nature.

TRADITIONS—Beliefs or customs that are handed down from generation to generation.

Places to Go

ON THE ROAD

BOSTON BRUINS
100 Legends Way
Boston, Massachusetts 02114
(617) 624-2327

THE HOCKEY HALL OF FAME
Brookfield Place
30 Yonge Street
Toronto, Ontario, Canada   M5E 1X8
(416) 360-7765

ON THE WEB

THE NATIONAL HOCKEY LEAGUE   www.nhl.com
  • *Learn more about the National Hockey League*

THE BOSTON BRUINS   bruins.nhl.com
  • *Learn more about the Bruins*

THE HOCKEY HALL OF FAME   www.hhof.com
  • *Learn more about hockey's greatest players*

ON THE BOOKSHELF

To learn more about the sport of hockey, look for these books at your library or bookstore:

  • Keltie, Thomas. *Inside Hockey! The Legends, Facts, and Feats that Made the Game.* Toronto, Ontario, Canada: Maple Tree Press, 2008.

  • MacDonald, James. *Hockey Skills: How to Play Like a Pro.* Berkeley Heights, New Jersey: Enslow Elementary, 2009.

  • Stewart, Mark and Kennedy, Mike. *Score! The Action and Artistry of Hockey's Magnificent Moment.* Minneapolis, Minnesota: Lerner Publishing Group, 2010.

Index

PAGE NUMBERS IN **BOLD** REFER TO ILLUSTRATIONS.

The Team

MARK STEWART has written over 200 books for kids—and more than a dozen books on hockey, including a history of the Stanley Cup. Mark got to know the Bruins well as a young fan. They were the arch rivals of his hometown team, the New York Rangers. He still has nightmares about Bobby Orr and Phil Esposito! Mark comes from a family of writers. His grandfather was Sunday Editor of *The New York Times* and his mother was Articles Editor of *Ladies' Home Journal* and *McCall's*, and also wrote for *Sports Illustrated*. Mark has profiled hundreds of athletes over the last 20 years. He has also written several books about New York and New Jersey. Mark is a graduate of Duke University, with a degree in History. He lives with his daughters and wife Sarah overlooking Sandy Hook, New Jersey.

DENIS GIBBONS is a former newsletter editor of the Toronto-based Society for International Hockey Research (SIHR) and a writer and editor with *The Hockey News*. He was a contributing writer to the publication *Kings of the Ice: A History of World Hockey* and has worked as chief hockey researcher at six Winter Olympics for the ABC, CBS, and NBC television networks. Denis also has worked as a researcher for the FOX Sports Network during the Stanley Cup playoffs. He resides in Burlington, Ontario, Canada with his wife Chris.